JOSHUA
and the Promised Land

Contemporary Bible Ser
JOSHUA and the Promised La
Retold by Joy Melissa Jens
Published
Scandinavia Publishing House 2c
Drejervej 15,3   DK-2400 Copenhagen I
Denm.
E-mail: info@sph
Web: www.sph

Text copyri
© Scandinavia Publishing Ho
Illustrations copyright © Gustavo Ma.
Design by Ben A
Printed in Ch
ISBN 978 87 7247 5C

JOSHUA
and the Promised Land
Retold for Children

by Joy Melissa Jensen

scanpinavia

Contents

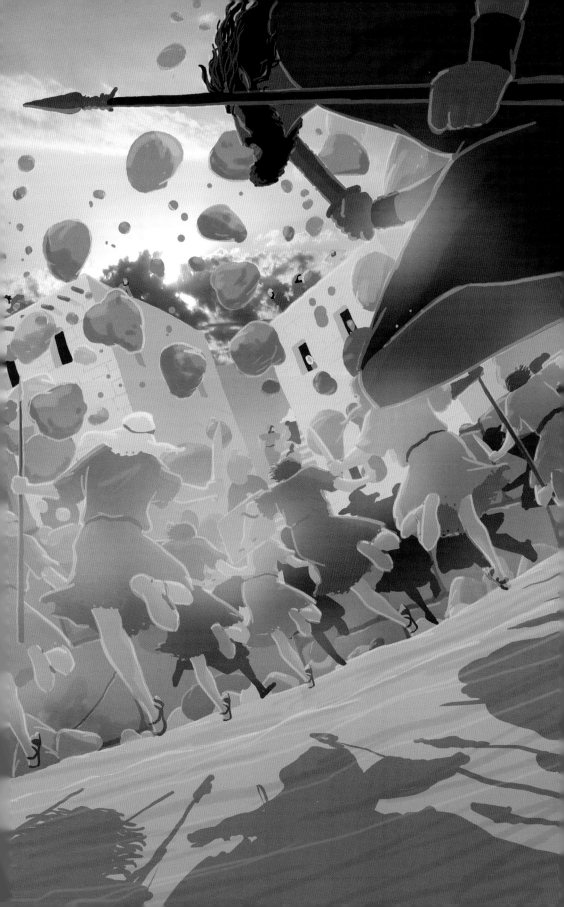

The Second
Ten Commandments

Exodus 34:1-9

God told Moses, "Be ready in the morning. Come up to Mount Sinai and bring two stone tablets with you. I will write the Ten Commandments on the tablets like the first ones that were broken. But don't bring anyone with you."

Moses cut two stones. Then he carried them up to the mountain The Lord came down in a cloud and stood beside Moses. "I am

the Lord," he said. "I love my people and I forgive their sins."

Moses bowed to the ground and prayed, "God, if you are pleased with me, go with us. Let us be your people."

God replied, "I promise to be with you. And I will perform miracles for you. The people in your land will see my great works and know that I am the Lord." Moses re-wrote the Ten Commandments in stone. He stayed on the mountain for forty days before coming back down to the people of Israel.

The People Grumble About Being Hungry

Numbers 11:4-15

The people of Israel left their camp at Mount Sinai. But they had not traveled very far before they began to complain again.

"This Manna bread is getting boring. Where is our meat?" they whined. "We might've been slaves in Egypt, but at least we had fish and garlic and melons."

The Lord heard everything they said. They were not thankful for

the food he gave them. "God," Moses prayed, "My people keep whining for meat. But where can I get it for them? You made me responsible for all these people and yet they're not my children. How am I supposed to help them?"

God answered Moses, "Tell the people not to worry. I have been among them and heard them complain. Tomorrow they will get more meat than they could ever eat."

The Lord Sends Quails

Numbers 11:31-35

God sent a strong wind over the sea. The wind carried a whole flock of quail into Israel's camp. There were so many birds that they began to land on top of one another until they were piled up three feet high. The people rushed around trying to get as much as they could. They stuffed them into bushels. They took the biggest quails and roasted them. But before they could sink their teeth into the meat, God's anger shook the camp. He had been watching the people's greedy ways. Some had not thanked God before they began to eat. Others complained they had no wine or fruit to eat with it. So the Lord sent a disease into the camp to punish the people. The ones who had been selfish died. The others buried them. They called the place "Graves for the Greedy." Then they packed up their camp and traveled on to a place called Hazeroth.

9

Miriam and Aaron Are Jealous of Moses

Numbers 12:1-15

Moses was a humble servant of God. He never thought he was better than anyone else. But his brother and sister were jealous of him. Miriam and Aaron gossiped about Moses behind his back. "Who does Moses think he is?" they said, "Why does he get all the glory?"

The Lord heard them say these things about their brother. He was disappointed and called them at once to the sacred tent. God came down in a cloud and stood before them. "I am the Lord," he said. "Moses is my servant and the leader of my people. He has been faithful to me. Why are you putting him down?" Then God left, but he was angry.

Aaron turned to Miriam and stepped back in fright. She had turned as white as snow. The Lord had given her leprosy. Aaron ran to Moses. "Brother!" he cried, "We have talked badly about you. But don't let God punish us for the foolish things we've said. Save Miriam from this horrible sickness."

So Moses prayed to God, "Please forgive my sister and heal her."

God answered, "I will do as you say. But first you must make her stay outside the camp for seven days as punishment."

So the people of Israel stayed at their camp for seven days until Miriam returned.

11

Twelve Men Are Sent into Canaan

Numbers 13:1-24

God told Moses to choose one leader from each tribe of Israel. He told Moses, "Send the twelve men ahead to explore the land of Canaan. This is the land I am giving to you and to the people of Israel."

So Moses chose twelve men. "Find out everything you can about Canaan's land," Moses instructed them. "Return and tell us about the land and the people. And bring back some fruit so we can see how well things grow."

The twelve men agreed and left for Canaan. As they went through the Southern Desert, the scouts came to the town of Hebron. They found three tribes living there. Then they went to a valley with huge vineyards and trees bursting with fruit. The men cut off a bunch of grapes. The bunch was so heavy and full of juicy purple grapes that two men had to carry it! They also took some pomegranates and figs. They called the place "Bunch Valley."

The Twelve Men Return

Numbers 13:25-33

After forty days of exploring the land of Canaan, the twelve men returned back to camp. "Canaan is an amazing land," they told the people. "Just look at the size of this fruit!" The men passed around the grapes they had brought with them. "But the people there are strong, and the cities have high walls all around them. There are tribes living along the sea, and down in the valleys and all over the desert."

The people began to worry. "How can we capture this land?" they asked each other. "There are too many people living there already." But Caleb wasn't worried. He was one of the Israeli leaders. "Let's take the land," he said. "I know we can do it!"

"There is no way we can take the land," the twelve men told him. "We saw the people there, and they are like giants. They were so big that we felt as little as grasshoppers."

Moses Speaks to Israel
Deuteronomy 8:1-18

Moses heard the people doubting, so he spoke to them: "Don't you want to go into the Promised Land? Have you already forgotten how your God has led you through the desert full of snakes and scorpions? He wanted to test your faith, so he made you go hungry. But he never left you. He sent Manna bread from the heavens for your hunger. Then he poured water out of a rock for your thirst. God knows that his people need more

16

than food and drink to live on. So he gave you the precious words he spoke. He is bringing you to the land he has promised your ancestors. It is a land with wheat and barley, and vineyards and orchards. We have already seen the size of the fruit that grows there. There will be plenty to eat and drink! But after you have had your fill, don't be proud. Don't forget you were once slaves in Egypt. The Lord was the one who set you free. The Lord gives you strength."

The Last Days of Moses

Deuteronomy 34:1-10

The people journeyed onward and camped at a place called Moab.

God led Moses on ahead across the Jordan River, while the others stayed behind. He took him to Mount Nebo. From the top Moses could see far and wide across the horizon. He could see the cities in the north. He could see the Mediterranean Sea far out west. And he could see the valleys in the South. Then God said to Moses, "This is the land I promised Abraham, Isaac and Jacob I would give to Israel. I have let you see it. But you cannot enter into it with your people. Now it's time for you to come and be with me."

So Moses died in Moab. He was a hundred and twenty years old. Israel stayed at their camp and wept for Moses for thirty days. He had been their leader, and God's special servant. No one ever forgot the amazing things Moses did for Israel.

Joshua Becomes the Leader of Israel

Joshua 1:1-9

Joshua had been Moses' special helper. God came to Joshua and said, "Now that Moses is gone, you must lead the people across the Jordan River into the Promised Land. Wherever you go, I will give you that land."

Then God said, "I will be with you, just as I was with Moses. Be strong and brave. Remember what Moses taught you. Read the Book of Law and obey my words. Think about what my words mean, and try to understand them. If you obey me, there will be no reason to be afraid. I will be there to help you wherever you go."

So Joshua became the new leader of Israel.

The Eastern Tribes Promise to Help

Joshua 1: 10-15

Back at the camp, Joshua prepared the people to march into the Promised Land.

"Pack plenty of food," he told them. "In a few days we will cross the Jordan River. On the other side is a land of riches, and God has promised to give us this land!"

Then Joshua met with the leaders of the Eastern tribes of Israel. He said to them, "God has given you the land to the east of the Jordan River. Your land is peaceful, and you can settle here right away. But the rest of us still have to fight off the people living in our lands. And since we are one people, we hope you will help. Then God will give us all peace."

The Eastern tribes gave their word to Joshua and promised to help.

Rahab Helps the Spies

Joshua 2:1-7

Joshua sent two spies into Canaan to the town of Jericho. They met a woman there named Rahab. She loved God and she let the spies stay in her home. But someone found out about them. "Some Israeli men have come to spy on us," they told the king of Jericho. "They are staying in Rahab's home."

So the king ordered his soldiers to go and arrest the men. The soldiers found Rahab's house and knocked on her front door. But Rahab had been clever and covered the spies up underneath some leafy plants. Then she went and opened her door.

The soldiers said, "Where are the spies you've been hiding? We have come to arrest them."

"They were here," Rahab replied. "But they left already. If you hurry you may be able to catch them."

So the soldiers went away and searched the road near the Jordan River.

24

25

Rahab Asks a Favor
Joshua 2:8-14

Meanwhile back in Jericho, Rahab told the spies, "The soldiers are gone! You can come out now." Then she told them, "I know that God has given Israel this land. He rules the heaven and earth. Everyone in Jericho has heard how God parted the Red Sea. And everyone knows that God led your people out of Egypt. Now they shake with fear because you are coming. But when the day comes for you to take Jericho, please remember my family. Treat them with the same kindness that I have treated you."

The spies replied, "If you keep quiet, we will do as you have asked. We won't harm your family, and may God punish us if we don't keep our promise."

The Spies Escape

Joshua 2:15-24

Rahab tied a red rope from her upper window. It ran all the way down to the ground below. She told the two spies, "Use this rope to lower yourselves down. You must leave quietly, and then go hide in the hills. The king's soldiers won't find you there.

They'll give up and come back to Jericho. Then you'll be safe."

The spies thanked Rahab and began to lower themselves down. But before they did, they turned around and said to her, "When our people take Jericho, leave this red rope hanging in your window. Then we will remember not to harm you or your family inside." Rahab agreed.

The spies left Jericho and hid in the hills for three days. And the soldiers never found them. When the spies returned to the camp, they told Joshua and the people of Israel everything that had happened. "The people of Jericho are frightened," the spies said. "They know the Lord is with us!"

The Sacred Chest Leads the Way

Joshua 3:1-7

Early the next morning, Joshua and the Israelites left their camp and traveled to the Jordan River. They camped by the banks of the water. The leaders went around and gave instructions to the people. "We will march into Canaan and into the city of Jericho," they told them. "The priests will carry the sacred chest, and everyone else will follow behind them." Then Joshua told them, "Keep your eyes open! The Lord is going to do some amazing things for us today." Joshua told the priests to carry the sacred chest into the Jordan River. They obeyed and lifted the sacred chest up on their shoulders.

Then the Lord told Joshua, "Today I will show the people you are their leader! They will know that I am with you, just like I was with Moses."

31

Israel Crosses the Jordan River

Joshua 3:9-18

"Listen to what your Lord God will do," Joshua told the people. "God will show you his power. There are tribes on the other side of this river. But the Lord will force them out of the land. Just watch what the Lord is about to do right now! As soon as the priests carry the sacred chest into the water, the water will stop flowing and pile up."

So the priests carried the sacred chest into the water. And just as Joshua said, the water stopped flowing and piled up. The men walked out into the middle of the dry river. Then the people of Israel crossed over to the other side. The people rejoiced!

Israel had finally reached the Promised Land.

34

The People
Set Up a Monument

Joshua 4:1-9

God told Joshua, "Have one man from each tribe find a large rock in the middle of the dry riverbed. Carry the rocks to the place where you will camp tonight. Then set up the rocks as a monument to this day. Someday your children or your grandchildren might come here and stumble upon them. You can tell them the story of how God dried up the river and led his people into the Promised Land."

Joshua obeyed and chose twelve strong men, one from each tribe. They picked out the biggest rocks they could find. Then they carried the rocks to their camping spot.

Joshua had the men build another monument. They put twelve large rocks in the place where the priests had stood in the middle of the dry riverbed. And it's still there today.

The Battle of Jericho

Joshua 6:1-14

The people of Jericho knew that the Israelites were coming. They stayed in their houses, shut the windows and locked the doors. All the while, Israel marched closer to Jericho.

God told Joshua what to do.

"March slowly around the city one time everyday," he said. "Do this for six days. Carry the sacred chest in front of you, and have the priests hold trumpets. Then, on the seventh day, march seven times around the city. Blow the trumpets and shout! I will let you defeat the king of Jericho

and his entire army. All the walls will fall down, and you can run into the city from every side."

Joshua listened carefully to God's plan. And when they finally reached Jericho, Joshua told the people what God had said. The people agreed, so Joshua shouted, "Let's march!" The priests went in front carrying the sacred chest. Some of them held trumpets. Then the people marched behind them. The walls of Jericho towered above them, but the people trusted the Lord's plan. They marched around once a day for six days.

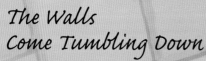

The Walls
Come Tumbling Down

Joshua 6: 15-27

On the seventh day, the people of Israel woke up
early. They began to march around Jericho. One, two,
three times they marched around the town. Then
four, five, six more times they marched. And on the
seventh time, Joshua called out, "Get ready to shout!
Let your voices carry up to God. He will let you
capture Jericho!"

   The people circled around one last time. But
this time the priests blasted their trumpets and
the people shouted up to the heavens, "Praise
God Almighty!" As they marched, the walls of
Jericho began to tremble and shake. Then the walls
crumbled and fell down. The people ran into Jericho
from every side. But they also kept their promise
and did not attack the house with the red rope in the
window. Rahab and her family were saved.

   And the Lord let Israel capture Jericho that day.

Joshua Commands the Sun to Stand Still

Joshua 10:1-27

The king of Jerusalem heard about Joshua and the battle of Jericho. He was afraid that Israel would capture Jerusalem too. He also got word that Israel had signed a peace treaty with the Gibeonites. The king knew that the people of Gibeon were great warriors. "What if the Gibeonites help Israel and attack us?" the king wondered.

So he decided to ask the Amorite kings for help. The Amorite kings attacked Gibeon and kept the people as prisoners. The people of Gibeon sent word to Joshua, saying, "Please come and rescue us! We've been attacked! Don't let us down."

Joshua and his army were faithful. They came and fought the Amorites and sent them running in all directions. Then the Lord created a hailstorm that wiped out their enemies. Joshua saw that the Lord was helping Israel. He prayed, "Lord, make the sun stop in the sky. Make the moon stand still. Do this until we have won over our enemies."

So the sun stood in the sky for a whole day until Israel had won the battle.

"We Will Worship and Obey the Lord"

Joshua 24:14-28

Joshua called the people of Israel together for a meeting. "Worship the Lord," he told them. "He is the reason we have won our battles. Don't forget to obey him, and be faithful servants. We are in a new land! The people here worship idols and false gods. Are you going to worship their gods? I'm not! My family and I will worship and obey the Lord."

The people answered, "We saw how God brought us out of Egypt. He protected us wherever we went. The Lord is our God and we will only worship him."

Joshua told them, "If you turn your backs on God, you will be lost. I know that some of you still have idols and statues. You must get rid of them and worship God alone."

Then Joshua set up a large stone under an oak tree. "Do you see this stone?" he asked the people. "This stone will be our witness if you ever turn against God."

The people promised, "We will only worship God." So Joshua helped the people make an agreement with the Lord that day. Then he sent everyone home.

42

43

Israel Settles in the Land

Joshua 21: 43-45

The Israelites settled in the land that the Lord had promised them. It was rich and beautiful, just like they had been told. Some of Israel's tribes settled in the valleys. Others settled along the sea. But wherever they went, God was always with them. They had good land to grow food, and plenty to eat. Their families grew and grew. Whenever the Israelites had to go to war, the Lord helped them win. He promised many good things for Israel, and he kept his promise every time.

Joshua's Farewell Speech

Joshua 23: 1-14

Joshua lived a long time. He was a good leader. While he was alive, Israel lived in peace. Before he died, Joshua called together a meeting with the leaders of Israel.

"The Lord has been good to us," he told them. "You have seen the things he has done and how he has fought for Israel. There are some enemies that still remain in our land. But God is faithful and he will give this land to

you. I have already divided this land between the tribes so that everyone will have something."

Then Joshua said, "I will die soon, just like everyone must. I will not be here to guide you, so remember to obey the word of God. Love the Lord, and remain faithful to your people. Don't be afraid. Any single one of you could defeat a thousand enemy soldiers, because God is on your side! He fights for you, and he keeps his promises."

Judah's Army Defeats Their Enemies

Judges 1:1-16

When Joshua died, the people of Israel had no one to lead them. They were preparing to go to battle with the Canaanites. The people prayed, "Lord, what shall we do? Which tribe should attack our enemies first?"

"Judah," the Lord answered. "I will help them take back the land."

Caleb was the leader of the Judah tribe. He called his soldiers together. Then he told them that the first man to defeat the enemy could marry his daughter named Achsah. The tribe of Judah went into battle with the Canaanites.

Othniel was a brave soldier of Judah. He captured the enemy town and won the battle for Israel. Just as he had promised, Caleb let Othniel marry his daughter.

After the wedding, Achsah told Othniel that he should ask her father for more land. He never did, so she went to see her father herself. As Achsah road up to the house on her donkey, Caleb could tell something was wrong.

"What's bothering you, daughter?" he asked her.

"I need your help," she replied. "The land you have given us is in the Southern Desert. It's hot and dry, there. Please give me some land with ponds, so that we can have water."

Caleb gave her a couple of small ponds named Higher Pond and Lower Pond.

49

The Lord Chooses Leaders for Israel

Judges 2:16-19

As the years passed, Israel became less and less obedient to God. They forgot about how the Lord led them out of Egypt. They forgot about how the Lord let Moses part the Red Sea. They forgot how the Lord let Joshua win the battle of Jericho.

And now they were forgetting God. But God had not forgotten them. He decided to put judges in charge of Israel. The judges reminded people of the Lord's almighty power and love. They also helped make decisions for the twelve tribes. They were fighters, too. Whenever enemies came and attacked Israel, the judges fought against them. Because the judges were obedient and good, the Lord always helped them win. As long as the judges were alive, the Lord let Israel live in peace.

51

Rescued by Othniel

Judges 3:7-11

God warned Israel that they would be tricked into worshiping other people's gods. And that's exactly what happened. They bowed down to idols, and they worshiped the gods of their enemies. This made the Lord was angry. So he let Israel be ruled by Syria for eight years. The Syrian king made the Israelites pay taxes. They were poor and miserable. They called out to God for help. God loved his people and he took pity on them.

He chose Othniel to rescue the people. The Lord's spirit took control of Othniel and he led Israel into war against the Syrian king. God let Israel beat their enemies. The people rejoiced and they lived in peace for forty more years.

God Chooses Ehud

Judges 3:12-20

After Othniel died, the Israelites disobeyed the Lord again. So he let king Eglon of Moab rule over the Israelites for eighteen years. He made the Israelites pay heavy taxes. The people prayed to God, and he answered their prayer. He forgave the people. This time he chose a man named Ehud to rescue the people from the king.

Ehud was an Israeli from the Benjamin tribe. One day the people sent Ehud to the king with their tax money. But before he left, Ehud hid a sharp dagger under his robes. He went to the king and said, "Your majesty, I have a message to you from God—but it's a secret." So the king sent all the servants out of the room.

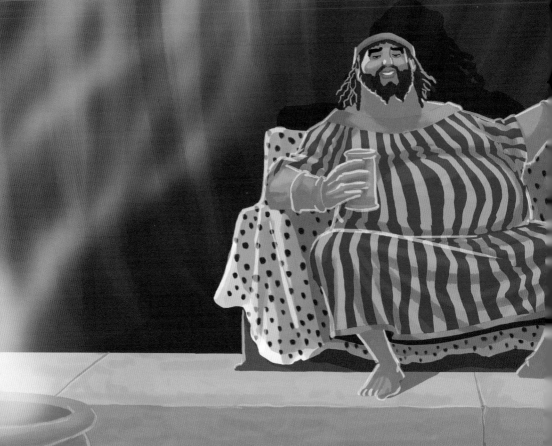

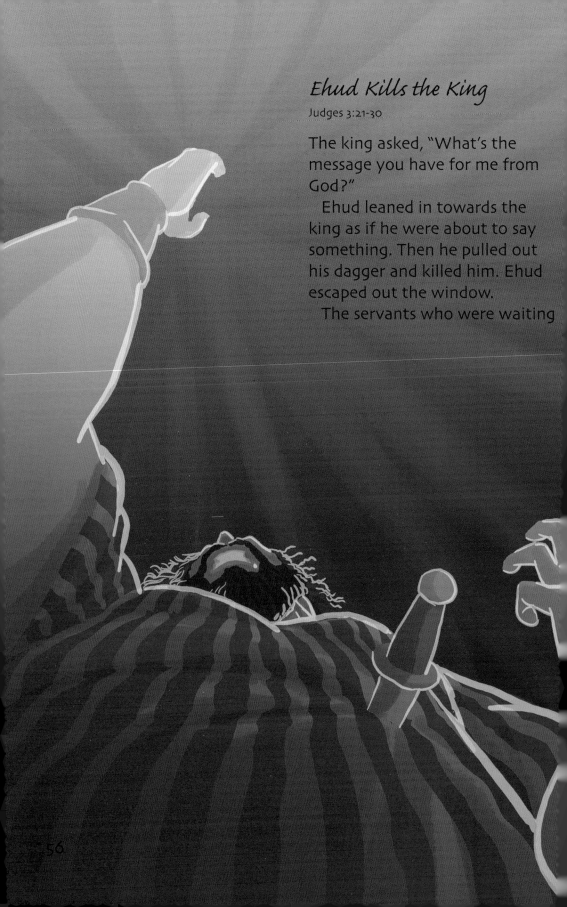

Ehud Kills the King

Judges 3:21-30

The king asked, "What's the message you have for me from God?"

Ehud leaned in towards the king as if he were about to say something. Then he pulled out his dagger and killed him. Ehud escaped out the window.

The servants who were waiting

in the hall began to worry. "What could be taking so long?" they asked each other. Finally they burst through the door, but all they saw was their dead king lying on the floor.

Ehud ran back to the Israelites. He blasted his trumpet and called the people together. They came out of their houses to see what was going on. "Follow me,"

Ehud shouted to them, "The Lord will let us fight the Moabites and win!"

So the people followed Ehud down to the Jordan valley. They fought their enemies and won. The people of Israel lived in peace for another eighty years.

58

Deborah and Barak

Judges 4:1-16, Judges 4:23

After Ehud died, the Israelites started to sin again. The Lord let the Canaanite king named Jabin capture Israel. Jabin had a great army. The leader of the army was a man named Siseria. He was tough and cruel to the Israelites. The people prayed for God's help.

At this time, Deborah was a special leader of Israel. Everyday Deborah sat under a palm tree. The people came to her with their problems and she would help them. The Lord had given her wisdom. She was a prophet of God, and sometimes God spoke to her and told her what to do.

One day Deborah received a message from God. She sent for a man named Barak to meet her under the palm tree. She said, "Barak, I have a message to you from God. Gather an army of ten-thousand people and lead them to Mount Tabor. The Lord is going to help you defeat the Canaanites. Our enemy Siseria will be there with his army. They may have fancy chariots and weapons, but we will have God on our side."

Barak said, "I will only go if you go, too."

"Alright, I'll go," said Deborah, "But don't expect to get any glory. Today the Lord is going to let a woman win against Siseria."

Then Barak and Deborah left to gather the troops.

The Lord Fights for Israel

Judges 4:10-24

Deborah and Barak led their army toward Mount Tabor. Siseria got word that Israel was preparing for battle. "Let's go," he called out to his soldiers, "The Israelites think they're going to beat us today!" The soldiers laughed and made fun of Israel as they climbed into their iron chariots.

Meanwhile Deborah told Barak, "The Lord has already gone on ahead to fight for us!" Barak led the troops down the

60

mountain. Siseria and his army were waiting below. During the battle, the Lord fought for Israel. He confused Siseria's army and made them afraid. They began to jump off their chariots and run away. Even Siseria tried to run away, but Barak's army ran after them. The Canaanites no longer had any power over Israel. That day Deborah and Barak sang, "Our Lord we pray that all your enemies will die like Siseria. But let everyone who loves you shine brightly like the sun at dawn."

Israel lived in peace for about forty years.

61

The Contemporary Bible Series